My Life

at
THE MARSHFIELD HILLS
GENERAL STORE

by

Sherry Campbell Bechtold

Published by Starboogie Press

Printed by Smith Print, Norwell Massachusetts

Cover design by David Brega

Cover photo by Dave Will
Back cover photo by Viola Khumen

For permission to use any portion of this book,
contact:

Sherry Campbell Bechtold
sherrybechtold@yahoo.com

ISBN: 978-0-615-85908-8

This book is dedicated to the gentle people of Marshfield Hills. I will carry you in my heart for the rest of my life.

Stories ~

Before ~

If you were to drive down Rte. 3A on the South Shore of Boston, you would pass through Hingham, Cohasset and Scituate, over the North River Bridge into Marshfield. You could easily keep going and completely miss any one of a few turnoffs to the left that would bring you into the Village of Marshfield Hills.

While house hunting in the late '90s, Fate whistled and called us to take one of those turns, directly into the heart of "The Hills", which later in 2010, became listed on the National Register of Historic Places.

To say this is a special place is obvious to anyone who has been here.

Today, the village looks a lot like it did in the middle of the 19th century. Large, gracious homes, some of which were once stores and a livery stable, still line Old Main, Pleasant and Prospect Streets, which meet at the crest of a formidable hill. In those farming days, there was a commanding view of the ocean, but that was before all the trees grew.

There are still lovely woods, streams, ponds and glacier ridges, much under the protection of the Audubon and Trustees of Reservation. Deer, red fox, weasels, rabbits, turtles, coyote and all manner of birds thrive in this little corner of heaven.

There are neighboring farms, the historic North Community Church and cemetery, the Grand Army of the Republic Hall, the Christian Science Church, Clift Rodgers Library and the Firehouse.

In the center of it all is a welcoming yellow building, with three doors and a long porch spanning the entire front. It was built as a general store in 1853 by Elisha Hall, a local businessman who lived across the street.

Today, the building is home to the Post Office, Marshfield Hills General Store, an upstairs apartment and an attic, which once was used for the sewing of Union Army, uniforms during the Civil War. The holes where the sewing machines were attached to the wide plank floors are still there.

For a time, at the turn of the 21st century, I had the opportunity to live in Elisha's house, run his store, experience life in a most extraordinary neighborhood and become part of its history.

ELISHA W. HALL.

Elisha Hall Obituary

ELISHA W. HALL. Late a retired merchant of Marshfield Hills, and a representative progressive citizen, departed this life a few weeks since, February 15, 1897, at his winter home, 259 Beacon Street, Boston.

Elisha W. Hall was well educated, having attended public and private schools in East Marshfield, evening schools in Boston, and in addition taken a special private course of study. His business experience was gained early; for at the age of fifteen he entered the employ of Mr. Elijah Stearns, a merchant in Boston. He was engaged as a clerk in Boston seven years, and then returned to Marshfield Hills or East Marshfield and entered the store that was formerly his grandfather's, but which the latter had sold a few years previously. He there managed a successful business until 1895, when he retired. Mr. Hall established a reputation as a wise and conservative businessman, and was Chairman of the Railroad Sinking Fund Commission from the time of its establishment. On October 29, 1854, he was united in marriage with Sarah, daughter of George H. Wetherbee.

Six children blessed their union, namely: Henrietta; Winthrop T., who has succeeded his father as manager of the mercantile business; Flora A.; Sarah B.; and two who have passed away.

Mr. Hall was Chairman of the Republican Town Committee of Marshfield for a great many years. Prior to the establishment of the Republican Party he voted with the Whigs; and he was Postmaster of East Marshfield for some time under the Whig administration. He was one of the prime movers in establishing the East Marshfield Public Library, and at the time of this death was a Trustee of that institution. He was appointed a Trustee of the Ventress Library Fund, and was so largely instrumental in the furnishing of the building and the collection of books that the whole may be said to be a monument to his energetic, prompt, and wise administration.

As a Free Mason, he was affiliated with Corner Stone Lodge, A. F. & A. M. of Duxbury. He was a prominent and liberal member of the Unitarian church of Marshfield, and was for years on the Standing Committee. The handsome residence at Marshfield Hills so long the home of Mr. Hall and his family, commands an enchanting view of sea and shore, and is one of the finest and most attractive places in this beautiful village.

Meant to Be

In 1996, my husband, Bob, and I were searching for a house on the South Shore of Boston when we saw a Realtor's ad for Marshfield Hills, only a couple of miles from where we then lived, in Scituate.

Although we had both been in the area for years, neither of us had heard of, much less visited, this little village.

Intrigued, we ventured out over the North River Bridge, taking the first left onto Summer Street, up Prospect, into the heart of Marshfield Hills. At the top of the hill stood a large pink Victorian house. I took one look, and said, "That's my house."

Bob was not impressed. "It's not even for sale. Anyway, it's old and not on the water. It's too big. Look at all that lawn." To which I replied, "Whatever you say. But I'm telling you that's *my* house."

The following weekend while out with our Realtor, she told us about a house she wanted us to see. "It's been on and off the market. I know it isn't what you said you wanted, but it's – well, 'different'. You might like it." As we followed her car, she pulled up in front of the pink Victorian.

Bob looked at me, "I don't believe it!" I didn't even flinch, "I told you it was my house."

Of course, we bought it. This dream house was a beautiful, rambling, confident home, with a huge barn, a field and woodlands. We learned it had been owned, in the late 1800s, by one of the village's prominent leaders, Elisha Hall, and in fact the house had remained in the Hall family for decades.

Across the street from the house was the Post Office and the Marshfield Hills General Store, in times past called 'the Genny'; now everyone calls it 'the General'. This building was built by Elisha as his store, which he operated until his death in

1897, when his son took over the business. Though it had been one of many stores in the Hills, it was the only one still in operation. It touched me that the house and the store were still here, still holding their places for the man who loved them both.

For the next few years, I continued to commute into Boston for my work and, like other commuters, was gone much of the time. I didn't know any of my neighbors and knew practically nothing about the village. But, on weekends, I often sat on my front porch and looked across the street at that old building.

As I watched people coming and going, into the Post Office to pick up the mail, buying a newspaper at the Store, I swear I could hear it calling my name. I kept telling Bob, "Boy, I would love to own that place." Every time I walked in there, stepping on those old floorboards, sensing the spirit of the Store's history, I couldn't help but imagine how it would be, if it were mine.

Then in 2000 just before Christmas, the Store suddenly closed and shortly after, we heard the entire building was for sale. Bob initiated conversations with the current owner and learned that there were two other couples in the neighborhood that were also interested – the Singers and the Shrands.

We all shared a desire to preserve the building's historic value and keep it from becoming a residence or business offices of some kind. So, in what seemed like no time at all, we joined forces and purchased the building.

I would rent the store space and create the business I had imagined. I couldn't wait!

I had my house. I had my store. It felt right. For the first time in many, many years, I felt like I was home.

Candy

As much as I wanted this Store, and as excited as I was to get started, the truth is I had no idea what I was getting myself into.

The time between the purchase of the building and the actual opening of the Store was all a blur of setting up bank accounts, researching vendors, painting shelves, finding displays that suited my idea of 'country store'. I know we must have eaten, but I doubt it was anything I cooked! Thinking about it now, I have flashes of waking up in the middle of the night with new inspiration – WE NEED A POPCORN MACHINE! Then I'd be online at 3:00 AM looking for popcorn machines. I was crazy with ideas for what I wanted in the store – great coffee, fresh baked muffins, nostalgic toys, unique greeting cards, ice cream, helium balloons. A HOT DOG machine! And of course, there had to be plenty of CANDY.

For weeks, I ordered more stuff, and more stuff arrived. Since the Store was being renovated, everything got piled up in our front hall at home. Then, when that was full, boxes of stuff spilled over into the dining room, and the living room. I had a LOT of stuff!

When we finally got to the point where I could unload and display, I was a woman possessed. Honestly, I don't know when I have had so much fun.

Almost the last to be unpacked and set out was the candy. We had designed the Candy Corner to be exactly where some old timers had told us it used to be - back when they were kids. I had plenty of shelves and piled them up with every kind of candy I could think of, particularly the old fashioned kind that you didn't see every day. When it was all stocked, I stepped back and gazed upon my creation and saw that it was good.

Now, here's the thing. The very next day after we opened, I took a look at that Candy Corner and was stunned at how much had been sold. It looked empty to me. In only one day, I had to re-stock!

I remember thinking "You're kidding me! Already? I have to do it again?"

THAT was the moment my real education began - that moment, followed by thousands of moments of schlepping boxes, opening boxes, stocking shelves, taking empty boxes to the dump. And repeat. For the next seven years. I never worked so hard in my life, and I never loved a job more.

Candy Corner by Sally Dean

The Post

The renovation work was pretty extensive – floors refinished, walls painted, lighting fixtures replaced, cabinets moved. We put a lot of thought into the design; a small space, it needed to be effectively utilized, and I was pretty happy with how our plan turned out.

But there was this post – a supporting post that had been used to house electrical wires that serviced the sales counter. Necessary, yes, but it was right in front of the counter, near the cash register. About 10 inches square. What the heck? What an eyesore.

Well, it wasn't going anywhere so I put it to work. A row of racks for magazines on either side. Presto! Merchandising. I'm a genius.

Sadly, I never did sell very many magazines. But, as so many things in life that reveal themselves in their own good time, the post's real purpose – its "raison d'etre" - unfolded.

It was, in fact, *the therapy post*.

Over the years, countless friends and customers leaned against that post, lingering to tell some new story, complain about a spouse, fret over a child, expound religious fervor, and sometimes (very, very seldom) express political views. I say seldom because I really did not 'allow' the discussion of politics inside the store. If a conversation veered in that direction, I instructed the offenders to take it to the porch. I personally did not engage in political discussions because it seemed that people became offended or heated, or both. I wanted everyone to just get along. And, if they weren't going to get along, well, I didn't want it to happen on my turf.

This "no politics talk" policy held out until the Presidential election of 2008, when even I had such strong views I could not stay quiet.

And, yes, I had been right. People did get offended and/or heated. It became obvious that, as opinions were openly and vehemently expressed, some people were forever changed in the eyes of their 'friends'.

The store was becoming a political hotbed of dissent. So, I reinstituted the law, though damage had already been done.

With the subject of politics eliminated from the confines of the store, the post endured as a platform for more personal issues.

Friendships were formed. Family disputes were aired. Romantic confessions poured forth. Lives took new direction. Epiphanies were experienced. It was a very powerful post!

I'd like to believe that, years from now, when someone else is in charge, the post will retain its power. And, that disgruntled housewives and well-intended spiritualists will spend quiet times in the Store, leaning, cleansing their souls before whoever is there to perform absolution.

Who knows? There may even be political discussions, since the self-appointed 'conversation police' will have left the building.

I Need Help!

Hank

We didn't know it at the time we opened the Store, but we had actually inherited someone from the previous owner. Hank had been working the register for, gosh, I have no idea how long – since Elisha?

Hank was a retired insurance guy, as I recall. At one point, he told me how old he was and I remember being surprised because I thought he was much older. He wore his pants too big, and his belt was cinched tightly to hold them up.

More often than not, he, nodding and smiling, would look at me while I was talking, and I knew he had no idea what I was saying. I suggested he needed a hearing aid, but he said he had one - he just didn't like to use it. Must have been pretty peaceful, not having to listen to what was going on around him. He also couldn't see very well, although at some point after he had some minor heart issues, he returned to work and gleefully informed me "I can see now, since my heart attack."

Hank was Mr. Reliable. He opened the store at 6:30 AM. Never late. Made the coffee. Set out the newspapers. Started the Lottery machine.

Nothing fancy, but I was so grateful that I didn't have to get up in the 'middle of the night' to work that shift!

Everyone knew Hank – of course, since he had been there since before almost everyone else was born – and everyone had heard his story many times over. He would happily re-tell any tale from his past to anyone who gave him an ear, though. And, he never missed an opportunity to talk about his beautiful, intelligent and accomplished daughter, who was his pride and joy.

Wiesy

The kind and gentle spirit Wiesy (*Weezy!*) was an artist and an animal lover. Consequently, she had an uncanny ability to capture the personality, the individual spirit of an animal in her delightful drawings. I had her do portraits of our Golden Retrievers Skipper and Star and, to this day, they are some of my favorite artwork.

Wiesy was also a puppeteer and sometimes she brought in one of her puppets to entertain the customers.

But one of the most endearing things about Wiesy was, and is, her unfailing commitment to saving the wolves.

I probably would never have thought about it, as we don't have wolves in Marshfield. But, her fervor was so contagious that now I care about them too, and will sign just about any petition that comes my way on behalf of their salvation. I will never see a picture of a wolf without thinking of her.

Patty

Patty was a writer and freelance bookkeeper, working for Donna Green, a well-known artist and philanthropist, with a farm around the corner on Summer Street. When I discovered she was looking for a part-time steady gig, I snapped her up, and over the years have congratulated myself many times for that decision.

Patty was an astonishing worker and at her best on Arts Festival weekend, behind the counter, with a line of customers all the way around to the ice cream freezer. Without blinking, and without taking a bathroom break for hours, she just processed purchases and sent folks back out into the fray of the Festival. Like a machine!

She was a no nonsense kind of gal, always the one to make sure things were working according to plan and not at all shy about getting help from whoever was handy if she needed it. One day, I was away from the Store, and she had been dealing with our new air conditioner, installed directly over the front door.

As Patty tells the story, "It leaked continually, raining cold, nasty water on people as they came in. So I would periodically shut it off, wait until it got unbearably hot again, then turn it back on and hope for the best. As the day went on, it got more and more temperamental and particularly cranky (or was that me?), so when a tall teenage girl walked through the door, I asked her if she would put her hand up in front of the unit and tell me if she could feel any air moving.

'My dad will do it' she said, turning to the man walking right behind her. Turned out the girl was Chelsea, and Dad was Steven Tyler, who obliged cheerfully, reaching up and waving both extravagantly ringed hands back and forth in front of the unit. 'Nope, nothing. Call the repairman!'

I remember being in awe of the normalcy of it all, and I got a lot of mileage out of telling my friends that Steven Tyler was moonlighting at the General as a maintenance man."

Norton

Bob Norton. I always called him Norton – in the best Jackie Gleason imitation I could manage. I actually knew him from a long time ago, a different life. He and I had been in a production of *Sweet Charity* for the Duxbury Bay Players back in the late '80s. He was a musician - played the guitar and sang - and was part of a really nice vocal group that I admired - The Snugtones.

I don't know how he came to work for me at the Store. People just seemed to show up and stay. Here's the thing about Norton: he tells the most corny, stupid, gut groaning jokes I have ever heard. And he's got a million of them – memorized from who knows where. It's like he's some kind of bad joke jukebox – and you don't even have to put in a quarter. He just walks in the door and they come forth, whether you like it or not.

For instance: Ephus and Effie are walking down the street in Portland and Effie notices that Ephus is walking funny, looks down and sees that he has only one shoe. "Ephus, what happened? Did you lose a shoe?" Ephus responds "No. I found one."

See what I mean? Sometimes, I laugh. OK, I usually laugh. In spite of myself.

The Well

The Marshfield Hills General Store

The role of shopkeeper at the Marshfield Hills
General Store was like being the mayor, the baby
sitter, the dogcatcher and the shrink. We were in
the heart of the village. It was the gathering place,
the hub, the village well. There, commuters who
had been neighbors for years finally met. Everyone
brought their dogs in for a visit.

Kids used it as a meeting spot, standing by the
candy corner with cell phones at their ears, "Meet
me at the General."

It was everything I had hoped for and more than I could have imagined.

If I said there was never a dull moment in the store, I would be only slightly exaggerating. Customers used to say I should put up a video cam and just let it run. "A Reality Show called The Store", someone suggested. If we could have done that, I would edit some of my favorite scenes together into a "composite" day, and it might look something like this:

7:00 AM

There's a chicken on our porch. A live chicken. Why? I begin to ask around and learn that Donna Green is missing a hen from her Magical Moon Farm; I'm guessing it's the one on our porch. With a little help, we identify the pranksters who thought chicken-napping would be great fun and they get a small piece of my mind before they are escorted back to the Farm, chicken in hands.

8:00 AM

Dave Will stops in to talk about the Run for the Hills Road Race coming up Labor Day weekend. He wants to know if the Store will be a sponsor again and can they still use the front porch and parking lot for registration and get-together before the race.

The road race has become a big deal. Makes me realize there's a whole new generation moving in and that is very cool.

9:00 AM

Tom is on his way to pick up the mail at the P.O. He stops and opens the door just enough to deliver his joke of the day, "I'm reading this great book on anti-gravity. Can't seem to put it down."

Not even waiting for a reaction, he closes the door and continues along the porch. I see him grinning to himself as he goes by the window.

9:30 AM

George Bohsack stops in on his way up the hill to Bible Study. He just wants to tell me that Molly's dogs bark at him when he walks by – every time.

As he leaves, one of my favorite older gents comes in, like every day, to buy his copy of *The Boston Globe*. He usually keeps to himself, but today shares with me that this is the only time of the day he sees another human being.

10:00 AM

Charlie arrives on schedule. In 'uniform', he's peering over his gold-framed glasses, and wearing his soft brimmed hat and his zip up windbreaker.

His white Cherokee is parked in front and I can see his little dog hanging out the window. He whines pretty much the whole time Charlie is in the Store. "Can you play some numbers for me? Can you do it manually or do I have to fill out the form?" I tell him I have time to do it on the machine – no form necessary! "Gimme 3 numbers – 6, 8, 9 – for both games and back it up." He looks down at Star, my Golden, lying next to me behind the counter. "Hey – that dog is getting kind of old, isn't he? I mean SHE. Guess what? That dog wags her tail every time I walk in here. I think he likes me. I mean SHE." He loves Star. Everyone does.

He turns his attention to this morning's gambling. "So, what's the Big Game tonight?" I tell him it's 'small change' – only two million. "All right, gimme one of those." I generate his "quick pick" for tonight's game and ask him what he's going to do with all that money, if he wins. He plays along with the fantasy. "Guess what? I'll give it to my kids. What do I need it for? I got money. I'm just foolin' around!" He chuckles.

"All right, I'll see ya' later." He'll be back in the afternoon. To get a paper. See Star wag her tail. Share a little banter.

11:00 AM

I hear whinnying outside and the unmistakable clop of horses walking on pavement. Rick Larsen and his daughter Hannah 'pull up' to one of the granite hitching posts, still there from a time when they were used constantly, near the edge of the parking lot. They make Tai and Arrow comfortable, give them each a little love, and then saunter into the store.

Rick is a trainer and passionate about horses. He shares information and stories about them to our interested ears. "Safety first. That's what horses want. Then fun. They love to have fun! And coffee. Tai loves coffee!" He buys a cup to share with his fun-loving friend. Hannah gets a juice drink and treats for her Arrow then they head back outside.

There are a few folks out there cooing and petting the animals. They are patient with these humans and gently swish their tails. But their enormous liquid eyes are intent on Rick and Hannah coming back to claim them.

So lovely.

12:00 noon

A boy around eleven comes in, like he does every day, to buy candy or soda. He's unusually cheerful and seems to have grown a couple of inches since the day before. He announces "I have a job now. I have my OWN money." Very proud, and isn't that a wonderful thing!

1:00 PM

Little three-year-old Gus, two houses down, runs ahead of his mom, Janet, from the Post Office. He dashes around behind the counter and announces, "Sherry, look what I have!" He stands still and drops his pants to reveal his brand new boxer shorts. They're plaid.

2:00 PM

A few members of The Old Goats show up to tell me about their monthly 'meeting' at PJ's Restaurant. They're wearing their Goat lapel pins, and are all smiley and chipper. Roger Williams tells me they've spent the past couple of hours terrorizing one of the career waitresses there, and still have a little energy left over, so they're winding down by giving me a hard time.

They try to tell me that the Goats are a serious group of retired businessmen, but I remind them that just last month, I happened to be at PJ's with Claire for lunch, and discovered the Goats in one of the side rooms, whooping it up and having one heck of a time. I'm on to them!

3:00 PM

A few young boys are at the register. They are paying with bills that are all crumpled up; one is taking them out of his sneaker. They toss them over the counter at me. A little pile of filthy damp balls of money. I've seen it all before. But, on this day, I finally have had enough. "No, that is not the way you give someone money. You flatten them out nicely and hand them to me. I demonstrate. "Try it." They do. Not sure how much of an impression I've made.

The boys leave, and next in line is Joe, one of my regular grownups. He places his purchases on the counter, then takes out his wallet and makes a great show of flattening and smoothing his bills, then hands them to me with great ceremony.

Everyone's a comedian.

4:00 PM

Two girls – around twelve– are in a moral dilemma. They tell me they're meeting two boys the next day and have heard that they're buying gifts for the girls - necklaces. They don't know what to do. They should get THEM something - they feel - but what?

"Here's the thing with boys." I'm in the pre-teen advice business today. "If they give you something, you smile and say, 'Thank you so much, that is very kind of you,' and you give them NOTHING." They stare at me with widening eyes. "Is that true?" they ask, not really believing. "Yes, that is absolutely true." They ponder this. "We should come talk to you more often."

5:00 PM

Peter Lange, tall and handsome husband of beautiful and elegant Heide, arrives to tell me about their most recent trip to New York City. They're big opera fans and go to the Metropolitan often. He knows I used to live right around the corner from the Met, am also a big fan and not so secretly still long for the Big City. So, he makes a point of coming to see me upon their returns, to tell me about the performance and bring me a program. He never forgets.

6:00 PM

Linda is here to buy her bottle of wine for Floosie Night. She has her little dog Maggie with her. The Floosies are a group of four women of a certain maturity who gather once a month at one's house, order pizza, drink wine and find out what each other knows about happenings in the 'hood.

All major issues are discussed and resolved – world, local and personal. Neighbors spy them walking over to one house or another (they live within ½ block from each other) and they wonder: 'what do they talk about?' And why are they called Floosies?' They would be very surprised.

The Floosies are Marci Littlefield, Linda Sordillo, Claire Robinson and me.

I already have my wine for the evening's festivities. And my $10 for the pizza. I'll be heading to Claire's as soon as I close up for the night.

6:55 PM

I'm counting cash, closing out the charge machine and recording Lottery ticket sales. One of our sweet senior neighbors, Helen, comes in, visibly upset. Her husband has been struggling lately and she's been taking him to the doctor.

Today, as she was helping him into the house, leaving the car door open in her driveway, a car stopped in front of her house, an unfamiliar guy jumped out, grabbed her purse from her front seat and took off. When I ask her if she had money in the purse, she tells me around $40, but it's more about the scare than the money.

Things like this don't happen here.

Tomorrow morning we'll put a jar on the counter and everyone will pitch in to put back what has been lost – in cash, and in faith in humankind.

~~~~

Every day something memorable happens.

Something touching. Something sad. Something funny. People just being people.

I sometimes think there is a kind of magic spell over these few blocks, just like Garrison Keillor feels about Lake Wobegon where 'all the women are strong, all the men are good looking and all the children are above average.'

Sure, there's the occasional kid who tries to heist a soda. A guy who spends too much money on the Lottery. There are sad housewives, men who work too much, kids who skip school. I know all that, but still…

The Beautiful Girls

I always wanted a daughter. Oh, how I would have loved that! I would have bought her dresses – shoot, I would have MADE her dresses! And little pink coats.

She would have worn patent leather Mary Janes and tiny white socks with lace trim. She would have had a canopied crib. And, dolls! American Girl dolls with all the accessories. Tea parties, baking cookies. You get the idea. But no. I have been deprived. And, it looks like a granddaughter is unlikely. So my fate may be sealed.

Mind you, I have the most wonderful son that a mother could want. And, an amazing grandson. I'm not really complaining. Well, maybe a little.

Like the tone-deaf man who wants to sing and the clumsy woman who wishes she could have been a ballerina, I seem destined to remain unfulfilled in my little girl wishes.

I bring this up now because I have an admission to make – one of envy.

There is a wonderful young couple, Amber and Steve, in our village, who at the time I first opened the Store, were the proud parents of Lydia with whom I was completely enchanted. Oh my, she was the perfect little girl. Amber looked like a Talbot's model, and Lydia was a miniature replica. If Mom had a cardigan draped perfectly over her shoulders, Lydia had one too.

It was their regular routine to come into the Store, after picking up the mail at the Post Office. Lydia was allowed to choose a DumDum pop and bring it to the counter with her nickel. She knew to say 'thank you' in that teeny voice, wait for Mom to take the wrapper off her pop and with all the delicacy of a princess, begin the slow process of licking her pop. Was there ever a more adorable child? I was in love.

They would then leave through the front door and Lydia would shake the bells left on the doorknob since December and say "Merry Christmas." Teeny voice. Little round cherubic face, perfect little smile.

The bells stayed, and no matter the time of year, the ritual of bell ringing and "Merry Christmas" continued, reinforcing my smitteness almost daily.

A couple of years went by and this fortunate mother received the blessing of yet another little girl. Betsy. Now, I ask you: does that seem fair? Two girls? Each as delightful as the other. I loved seeing them all together. Lydia copying Mom. Betsy copying Lydia. To my eyes, idyllic.

I would greet them, "Ah, here are the Beautiful Girls!" They'd giggle.

Occasionally, Steve would come in on his way home from work and I rarely failed to tell him how lucky he was. "You do know that your family is the best part of you, don't you?" He would smile and nod. "I actually do." A very wise young man.

Since the writing of this story, I have gotten my wish! My son and his wife were kind enough to adopt a feisty, adventuresome, talented and intelligent little girl - Luna! I like to believe this was, at least in part, to make me happy.

I am.

The Artist

When I was still commuting into Boston, the only time I saw the neighborhood was in the evening, when Bob and I walked Skipper and Star up to the cemetery next to the North Community Church and back home again. The homes on Old Main Street might as well have been a movie set; everyone was indoors having dinner, putting children to bed.

On one cold mid-winter walk, as we passed the G.A.R. Hall, we noticed that the front door was open and the lights were on. Though there was a sign in front that said "North River Arts Society," we really had no idea what kind of activities went on there – we were not artsy folks. But the building is historic, the lights were on, and it seemed cozy in there, so we decided to take a peek.

"Hi," a warm male voice welcomed us as we entered the main hall. The voice belonged to a big guy – I guessed he had played football in college – in jeans and a plaid shirt.

Glasses, nice face. Obviously a friendly native, possibly a custodian.

After determining we were brand new to the neighborhood, he decided this was a perfect opportunity to demonstrate his significant knowledge of the history of the building, the Arts Society, events held here, and the fact that "once upon a time" there had been a theatre group that did productions on the small, rudimentary stage, but that, now, the building was completely dedicated to visual arts.

"You see that room?" He gestured to a second floor balcony type studio. "A very famous artist has his studio up there." We gawk. "Really? What's his name?" (as though we would recognize it.) "His name is David Brega. He paints trompe l'oeil and is internationally famous." He added, "Perhaps one of the greatest trompe l'oeil artists in modern art history!"

"Oh. Wow."

What the heck is trompe l'oeil? We were so impressed, even if we didn't know why. I think we were beginning to realize that we had moved into a really cool neighborhood, replete with famous artists, recording stars (we had heard there were rock stars here somewhere) and who knows what other life forms of glitterati.

"So, is this guy around all the time? Do you think we'll have the opportunity to meet him? Does he ever have any of his work here at the shows?" We were establishing our groupie status.

"Ummm. Well, actually, he's me. I'm David Brega." Big smile. The beginning of a long friendship.

Over the years, I got to see David daily - sometimes multiple times – on his way to the studio, coming in to get a half cup of coffee (that was all he wanted). Sometimes at lunch, we'd share a wrap from Morning Glories while he regaled me with stories about 'the boys' (his Aerosmith buddies – aha, there *are* rock stars in the 'hood!) or we'd talk about Western Mass., where we both grew up.

On my walks with Star, I often stopped in and visited him in that little studio upstairs in the G.A.R., catching up on what was happening with the current piece of Masonite on his easel. On one particular day, Star and I were the audience for David's big 'reveal plan' for his latest: "Founding Father."

Comfortable on the old beige corduroy sofa, with Rudy, David's sheltie with the white blaze that runs crooked down his dignified nose, we were rapt as he shared his vision for the upcoming show.

37

It was going to be a Production. He loves a production!

"So, listen to this." He pops in a CD, stands back and prepares to conduct. "Okay. So the house is completely dark." A few measures into the piece – the theme from Apollo 13 – "And now, you begin to see some backlighting on the stage, and then -- big crescendo -- the spot comes up on the easel in the middle of the stage, a huge American flag behind it. The lights slowly rise and (another big crescendo) TADA!" John Adams in all his Revolutionary splendor captured in a setting only David could have imagined.

"So, what do you think? It's great, right?" He is so excited.

"Yes, I think it's fantastic." I really do.

Our friendship with David introduced us to the Arts Society where a lot of amazing people teach and show their work. Over the years, we saw young and not so young artists blossom, show-by-show, Festival-by-Festival.

We learned about different mediums and styles, found favorites, developed opinions and of course, began to buy original art for ourselves.

The list of talented, dedicated and diverse artists in the Society was and is awe-inspiring. David had brought trompe l'oeil into our world and soon Ted Polomis was in his company.

We watched our friend Doug Aaberg follow a lifelong dream and become a wonderful oil painter. Liz Haywood Sullivan captivated us with her sublime pastels. And Mary Callahan with her Italy! Sergio Roffo's gorgeous coastal landscapes. Marcia Ballou's bright, whimsical florals. Jody Regan's Monhegan Island. Page Railsback's colors, Joreen Benbenek's glorious skies, Dot Krause and her extraordinary multi-media pieces, the photographic art of Mike Sleeper and J Michael Sullivan and oh, so many other artists that keep the organization thriving, all held together by the dedicated work of Laura Harvey at the helm.

How wonderful to have the NRAS in that little white building down the street as a constant reminder of human creativity and joy. Even if we aren't 'artsy', don't necessarily know what we're looking at, or have a clue as to how it is done, we can observe. We can begin to appreciate. We can be grateful for those whose gifts grace our lives.

The Grand Army of the Republic
G.A.R. Hall
Marshfield Hills
Home of the North River Arts Society

New Single Guy in Town

I know a lot of people believe that suburbia, if that's what we call where we live, is no place for single people. They think that everyone around here is Married With Children. Or at least Married. Not true. Actually, a fairly large number of people – of varying ages – who come into the Store on a daily basis are without partners. Almost without exception, they lament the "fact" that there are no single people around.

Why don't they know each other? How do we rectify this problem? Bring all the singles together so they will know they are not alone?

Oh, I've thought of the rather ordinary approach – a singles dance, or wine tasting party. Boring. I've wanted to come up with something really different, but lacking any cool ideas, have done nothing. For this lack of action, I feel a little guilty.

Maybe it's because they know I care, single men and women tend to tell me their stories. Well, actually, everyone tends to tell me their stories regardless of their marital status. I think I like the single folk stories so much because they have a tad more drama in them.

Married people can be so predictable. Single people live life on the edge! Pathos of loneliness one minute, all starry eyed and passionate the next.

A while ago, the neighborhood juices got flowing when a New Single Guy moved in. I remember well his arrival because it was the time for our annual neighborhood Spring Social. I always go to these things because, after all, it's a neighborhood event. But I don't really enjoy them because they're very crowded and noisy and I'm an old poop.

I was no less of an old poop at this particular gathering. In fact, I was getting ready to leave, having had my obligatory glass of white wine, and mingled about as much as I could manage. I was already getting hoarse from screaming over the DJ's ever increasing volume of music that was clearly two decades after my time.

Just as I was aiming for the door, and politely had placed my empty glass on the refuse tray, Kim Dwyer, our adorable and outgoing town yoga teacher grabbed me. "Come on, dance with us." Us being the 'girls' from our yoga class. Okay, well I like these women. What the hey?

So, I'm having a little fun now, me and the rest of the yoga girls, when Kim, being herself, drags into our circle this NEW SINGLE GUY.

Oh, he was definitely new. Somewhere in this 40's, good looking in a dark, Mediterranean way. Different enough to raise an eyebrow or two. "Who is this guy?" I ask subtly. "Oh, he's new," one of the girls announces. Well, yes.

As the weeks went by, the NEW SINGLE GUY – now Chris - started skateboarding down the hill, often shirtless (but who's watching) using the front of my Store as a launching place. Always a big smile and a 'happy to be here' vibe, he eventually became a favorite Post Leaner. Very few topics were off limits.

"Hi. How're things here?" Chris strolls into the store wearing his usual crisp white long sleeve button down shirt and black jeans. Makes him look really tan, and his hair really black.

I smile, "Same. Haven't seen you in ages. What's up?"

"I've been spending some time with my Mom in Boston. She's not well. But, I'm home for a while now." He dotes on his mother and that touches me.

I tell him that Kim had asked about him the other day, wondered about how he's doing. "Huh. That is funny. I just saw her a few minutes ago and for some reason I blurted out that my girlfriend was moving in with me. Why would I just tell her that? Weird."

I don't think it's so weird. "Maybe because she's always trying to fix you up with women?" He knows it's true, but doesn't say anything, just looks up at me through thick lashes. "So, where's this girlfriend now? " I ask because I'm obviously nosey.

"Oh, she's on her cell phone in the car. I'm just passing time until she's done." He's decided to change the subject. "You know, I was wondering about Steven (Tyler). How is he?" I fill him in, "He was just here a few minutes ago. He has a toothache."

"I love this place." He smiles and shakes his head. "Well, I might as well buy something while I'm waiting." He wanders off.

A couple of boys come to the counter to pay for Cokes and Doritos. They've been swimming at the dam in the woods and their money is soaking wet. Well, I'd prefer that kind of wet to sweaty money from inside some kid's sneaker.

You'd be surprised just how often that actually happens.

The wet boys leave and Chris is back. He gingerly places a can of whipped cream on the counter. He has a funny look.

I don't want to ask.

"We've got a couple of hours to kill. Why not?" He is not even a little embarrassed.

A couple of hours. Who is he kidding?

The Morning After

Every Memorial Day weekend, our quiet little village expands exponentially and becomes a magnificent, multimedia feast for the senses: world class paintings, sculpture, photography, unusual artisan crafts, plants and poetry, music, clowns, face painting, popcorn, hot dogs and hamburgers, cotton candy.

The North River Arts Society Festival for the Arts all begins with the Gala Opening Party on Friday night, when attendees have the privilege of previewing the beautifully displayed artwork, enjoying hors d'ouevres, drinks and live music.

Saturday and Sunday bring out everyone else as the streets are closed off from traffic, and literally thousands of visitors descend upon the village, cars parked everywhere despite all the NO PARKING signs.

There's a live entertainment schedule both days that includes singing groups, bands, Alex Pevzner's exciting drum circle, and Paul McCarthy as our MC.

It's a scene of pure Americana. Norman Rockwell would have happily set up his easel to capture the images.

At the Store, we always hustle to gear up for Festival business, knowing that these two days will bring the biggest sales of the year. Since 1964, this event has been an annual gift from the Arts Society to its members, its artists, the village. Rain or shine, warm or cold, the show goes on. Then, all too soon, it's Sunday night and the Festival is over for another year.

On Monday morning, the crowds have all gone and you can hear the birds again on Old Main Street. This is the time for a different kind of celebration.

There's a small gathering of neighbors in front of the G.A.R. With the aid of the High School Band, a few of Colin McCauley's vintage cars, an engine from the Hills Firehouse, and members of the VFW in uniform, we form our annual parade to the cemetery up the hill.

Kids decorate their bikes – I remember doing that over a half century ago. Some families pull their tots along in Radio Flyers, their dogs with them, only to cover their sensitive ears later during the gun salute.

Once everyone arrives, there's a ceremony with memorial readings, sometimes a song, and a brief homily. It isn't glamorous, but this expression of respect for our heroes is close to the hearts of everyone here. It's a fine way to close a special weekend.

Today, on this particular Monday morning after the Festival, I'm walking back to the Store before the ceremony has finished. I need to get back to business. Behind me, up on the hill, I hear the gun salute. Now the bugler is playing "Taps."

Brad and Julie White's front lawn chairs sit empty after hosting visitors all through the weekend. The children's Art Tent is still in the driveway and chalk drawings have turned Old Main Street itself into a work of art.

Right here, Gary the Clown held a captive audience with his tricks and shenanigans, as he does every year.

I walk past the G.A.R., where a few folks have stayed behind to set out coffee and donuts for the parade participants. Some neighbors are sitting on their porches or standing about the empty booths and tents, chatting about the Festival - the winners of the juried art, Sophie Shrand who sang the National Anthem.

Across the street is Mitchells' barn, where a lot of non-juried original art was sold. Tables and chairs, festoons, streamers are all still in place, waiting to be taken down and put away until next year.

The big food tent spans the empty lot between the G.A.R. and the Littlefield's house. Marci and Walt will make good use of it later, hosting a cookout. Last year, they had a "hat theme" for the party. Claire won the prize when she, grinning like a self-satisfied cat, sashayed over from her house with an enormous butterfly on her head - so big, she looked like she might take flight. I still wonder where she found such a thing.

It's a gorgeous morning; we got lucky this year. The air still crackles with the high energy of Saturday and Sunday. There may even be echoes of laughter and jazz reverberating in the canyon of homes that line the street. But my ears are not tuned to that fine a vibration.

I love the Festival, but somehow this time - this morning after - is most precious of all.

The quiet. The peace that comes from jobs well done. The nurturing feeling of ties that bind having been gently tugged and tightened.

As I step onto the Store's porch, I realize I've been smiling for a long time. The atmosphere is so subdued, I'm aware of the sound of my footsteps on the wood porch floor. The large old windows displaying the darkness inside the Post Office. Lovingly protected old advertisements left on the wall from another century. Granite posts with their hitching rings.

I can hear the High School Band begin to play a Souza march - "Stars and Stripes" - as they start their walk back from the cemetery.

The door to the Store is propped open. Patty is at the Register. Someone's out of town relatives are looking at MHGS Tee Shirts for souvenirs. A neighbor is fixing a cup of Green Mountain coffee to his satisfaction and eyeing a muffin.

It's a wonderful scene. I can't imagine life getting better than this.

The Poet

"Poor Niky. I don't know what to do. That storm we had yesterday, I had to put him out in the car, the only thing that calmed him down. And, it's so warm, I hate leaving him out there. He just gets crazy with the lightning and thunder. It's like he's psychotic." Ray wags his head, gazes down, deeply dismayed and concerned.

It's Sunday morning and he's here to buy his *New York Times* - but only the Book Review and the Magazine sections - for $5.00. This troubles my Scottish blood. "You don't want the rest of it? Maybe give it to a neighbor? Use it for your fireplace? "

He shakes his head, still lost in his worry. "I brought him to the Vet. Again. She suggested Dramamine. But nothing… I don't know. My poor boy."

What can I do but listen?

"You know, I even took him to this specialist. She put Niky into a room and played CDs of thunder. I watched from the other side of a one-way mirror.

I think he fell asleep. No reaction. The doctor said she thinks it's me. She thinks Niky is responding to my anxiety. But I'm only anxious because he is. How does that work?"

I try again to comfort. "Well, that was only a CD – not the real thing. The real thing is accompanied by a lot of other occurrences. You know, barometric pressure, smells, flashing lights. Maybe it's not you." I'm trying.

"Yeah, I think it's me. Poor Niky." More head wagging.

I think about Ray's other dog. "What about Maizie? Does it bother her, too?" He chuckles. "No. Nothing bothers Maizie." Well, at least I got him to smile. Sort of.

Ray is more concerned about his dogs than anything else in his life. He won't travel because he doesn't want to leave them. He schedules his outings around their schedule: Carrots at 3:30. Dinner at 5:30. Bedtime at 9:30.

He is what one might call a Character. Colorful. Enigmatic. From the outside, in. Salt and pepper hair, which may or may not respond to the workings of a comb. Face weathered by smoking and thinking. Does he shave? Can't tell.

Jeans, not new and a tad too big, held up over Etruscan hips by a frayed belt. Flannel shirt in the winter with a thermal underneath. Unbuttoned short sleeve shirt in summer. No sartorial pretense here.

The pinky finger of his right hand is crooked, permanently bent from an accident. With that imperfect right hand, he writes poetry. I've asked him why he doesn't use a computer, but he waves off the idea. He wants to see his writing (which only he can decipher) on the yellow lined paper.

He seems interested in computers only to Google Search himself. He finds that utterly fascinating and likes to see how many references he has compared to his buddy, David Brega. At last count, he had a healthy lead. This pleases him enormously.

If you were to Google Ray Amorosi, you'd find numerous references to his poems and books, links to other renowned American Poets, biographies that talk about his teaching career and that he resides in Marshfield Hills. All that is just Cliff Notes.

Ray is a book you have to open and take the time to read. If you glance at the cover and think you know the story, you'll be so wrong.

You'll never know about his childhood in the North End, or his uncle who dragged him to art museums until he finally could *see* the color blue. And how that developed into a lifelong deep appreciation and collection of fine art.

How would you know that he loves liver with bacon and onions and periodically schedules visits to the Milepost Restaurant in Duxbury where it's still on the menu?

The biggest secret is that, if you're lucky and among the 'inner circle', you may be treated to his unrivaled tomatoes. The secret is lime, lime and more lime and that he hand pollinates his plants because "there aren't enough bees anymore."

He will tell you stories that you will absolutely believe are true. At a much later date, he confesses they're not. He just likes to try them out - heh heh….

He never forgets a kindness and he looks after those he loves.

Most people will never have the opportunity to know him but you will get a glimpse of the man's spirit through his work.

I'm patiently waiting for the publication of his next book with poems about Marshfield Hills. It's to be about his house - the Macomber House - and the amiable ghost who welcomed him there when he and his wife Peg first moved in. And about the marshes, the barns, the distant ocean you can hear from the top of the hill, his abundant garden.

Maybe there will be a poem about Niky and the thunder.

Next Register, Please

Brooks was one of the first helpers I hired for the Store. His mom, Molly, and dad, David, were two of our partners in the ownership of the building. He had two younger brothers, Ryan and Taylor, and the family lived right down the street. Brooks was a nice young high school kid, pre-driver's license age; I figured I could hold on to him for a little while. He helped out with stocking inventory, and he was great at the register. Customers liked him.

Brooks reporting to duty each day was announced by the sound of his skateboard on the porch ramp. None of the other neighborhood kids were permitted to do that. He had privileges. Stepping off the board, he'd flip it in the air and catch it, park it on the porch and walk through the front door, walking directly to the CD player to change the music.

He disapproved of my old-fashioned rock 'n roll, but was always willing to compromise. Something he could tolerate, something I wouldn't find unnerving.

On the rare occasion of a standoff, we could always agree on Bob Marley. "Ev'ry little thing is gonna be alright!"

Brooks loved his music and wanted to learn guitar. When he told me he was thinking about taking lessons from my own teacher, the notorious Gerry of Scituate Music, I had misgivings. I told him, "Gerry is an amazing musician, but he can be cranky, irascible, overbearing, with has a well-deserved reputation for being hard on students."

Undaunted, Brooks was off to his interview with the demon guitar teacher. Next day, I was curious. "What happened?" He admitted that Gerry eyed him with skepticism, yet another flighty teen who wants to play guitar. Finally he crossed his arms in front of his chest and issued his warning, "You know, you have to work at this. This takes practice. A LOT of practice. This requires a commitment." Brooks said he knew.

As it turned out, he was very committed, and very serious. He just soaked it all up like it was the most natural thing in the world, quickly learning riffs, making up his own, playing and singing along like he'd been born with a guitar slung around his shoulder.

The highlight of his week was his lesson with Gerry, and on his way, he'd stop in at the Store, grab a ginger ale and bag of popcorn for Gerry, while Mom waited in the car.

He was one of those kids. He was the real deal. A genuinely nice guy, smart but not overly intellectual, funny without being goofy, gentle and kind, but very much a guy. If you had a daughter, you'd want Brooks to be her boyfriend.

Life was just so darned much fun for Brooks. He knew how to juggle! It was not unusual for him to go around the Store, pick up a few different items and set them spinning into the air, with the most devil-may-care expression in his cool blue eyes.

In an easy attempt to drive me crazy, he liked to do this with bottles or cans of soda -- so that stocking the coolers was a bizarre form of entertainment. If I offered to help, he'd flip a few cans in the air, then say, "Catch!" as he tossed them to me one by one to place in the cooler. It was really mesmerizing to watch him do this. And a little terrifying too, waiting for one of those cans to explode. But, magically, that never happened.

When I left him alone at the counter, I was often rewarded by a variety of Brooks' creations: crossword puzzles on the candy bags, "portraits" of me taped to the register, or under the counter glass - not particularly flattering - but funny.

One afternoon, I came back from a break to find him quietly reading behind the register. There was a sign in front of him that read "Next Register Please". Without even looking up, he turned the sign around and on the back it said "I'm Not Kidding". And then there was self-promotion: "Vote for Your Favorite MHGS Employee" - everyone else's name in tiny print, but BROOKS was shamelessly spelled out in very large letters across the paper.

Molly said he had the warped sense of humor characteristic of her side of the family and loved to tell me about his antics at home. How they would watch TV in separate rooms -- something like "Whose Line is it Anyway" -- and call each other on their cell phones to laugh together about some routine.

Mom was the quirky nurturer and dad was the adventurer, always making sure to take each of his boys somewhere exotic – just the two of them. On one lovely late summer afternoon, Brooks dashed through the store to grab a coke.

"I'm going to Peru!"

He and his dad were airport bound to begin a trip they had planned for some time. He was so excited!

As he sailed past me and out the door, he sang out "Ciao!" That was how he always left it with me and he would refuse to leave until I said it too. "See you later" or "Bye" didn't cut it for him. So it was "Ciao, Brooks." He was gone.

A little over a week later, he and his Dad returned from Peru late on Saturday afternoon. A little time left to the day, the whole family went to the Marshfield Fair together. That night, Brooks went to his room and talked with his girlfriend on the phone before going to sleep.

Sunday morning, his Mom made breakfast in the kitchen below his room. As the bacon was crisping, she called up to Brooks to come down. When he didn't answer, she climbed the stairs.

On that same Sunday morning, I came home from church, and sat down in the kitchen for a cup of tea. It was an absolutely gorgeous day – just a hint that autumn was knocking at the door. Bright, quiet, peaceful. Then, out in the street, I heard the most horrific howl – coming from a person? "NO! God, NO!" That was all.

I sat in my chair, waiting. The phone rang but I didn't answer. I knew something awful had happened. I wanted to hang on to ignorance as long as possible.

In moments, Bob walked through our back door, ashen, hardly able to speak, almost without air to form the words. "I don't know how to say this. Brooks has died." There it was. The bomb I knew was coming my way. I just hadn't known the name on it would be Brooks.

Of course, I couldn't believe it. How? When? In Peru? Had he gotten sick there? Was his Dad also gone? No? Last night? In his sleep? How? Why? No. Not Brooks. Not Brooks. Not Brooks.

As I struggled with this new reality that I just couldn't get my mind around, Bob said, "You have to pull yourself together. You need to get down to the house. Molly needs you." Of course.

The following days were... well, they were terrible. I posted myself at the store, and had the burdensome task of breaking the news to neighbors who came in, many who were returning from vacations. We had a picture of Brooks on the front door that said, "We will miss you" under it. People took it hard. Most just simply broke down as they came through the door.

It was all an agonizing nightmare of tears, helplessness and the empty 'why.'

The funeral at the Community Church was overwhelming. No places left to sit or stand inside, people gathered around the church, watching and listening through the open windows. Gerry came and played his guitar. Beautiful things were said about a boy we all loved. Devastated, we all struggled to let go. We went to the cemetery, and a mother and father buried their oldest son.

It's been years now. And, yes, the miracle of life is that it goes on - even when we think it's impossible. Even when we really don't care or want it to - when we, left behind, are dulled by shock, bad dreams and unanswered questions. They never did determine exactly what happened inside his body that night.

What do you do when loss is unbearable? The best you can do is try to create beauty and meaning from your grief. His parents established a travel program at the high school in his name, got the village playground named after him, planted a butterfly garden.

Wiesey did a rendering of Brooks behind the register with his baseball hat, sheepish grin and that "Next Register Please" sign in front of him. For a long time, the original drawing hung in the store, then it moved to its permanent home In Molly's dining room.

The silly little signs and pictures he had drawn for me became priceless treasures.

If I had known, as he was dashing out the door with his Coke, what would I have said? Thank you? There's no one else like you? It's an honor knowing you? The world will be a darker place without you?

These are all imaginings of a broken heart. I am simply grateful for having seen his smile, met his eyes and had the opportunity to say "Ciao".

"For some, it's the tiny memory that pins down a boy on the invisible map of loss. Yet, something lingers in the mind, in the store. Perhaps the duffel bags left in the driveway after a long trip, for someone else to pick up? The hand that passes a few bills in change over the glass counter. The turn of a shoulder as youth itself walks down the hill to a yellow house with children, dogs, parents - everything ready for life, but the bags tell of another journey, which never yields. Yet something lingers in the very center of the flesh, never forgotten in the mind, the store, down the hill leading home."
~ Ray Amorosi

"Brooks" by Wiesy MacMillan

Thanksgiving

Autumn was difficult in our little village. Everyone was still in mourning, even - or especially - as we approached the holiday season. Of course, like any other community, we had our share of challenges and sadness. Dogs went missing, couples divorced and households broke down. Kids got into trouble. Favorite neighbors found new jobs and moved away. Beloved ministers moved on to new parishes. Occasionally, we said goodbye to a dear widow.

And, we moved on.

But, this was different. This dense fog of sadness would not dissipate. He was just a boy - such a special boy - gone in the blink of an eye, with no explanation to help us find acceptance.

Our hearts ached for ourselves and for his family, particularly Molly, who knew everyone in town and did so much for others. We all would have done anything to spare her this wrenching grief, but there was nothing to do but be her friend and hope that somehow she would eventually find her smile again. In truth, it seemed we had lost her as well as Brooks.

Remarkably, the earth continued to rotate on its axis. A painfully beautiful September came to an end and slid effortlessly into the kind of October we brag about in New England. But, the red and gold autumnal extravaganza didn't fit with the pall of heartache that had settled in among us. It was a mercy when the trees turned into black skeletons against a background of drizzle.

Of course, I continued my daily routine at the Store. That's what you do - put one foot in front of the other, doing the day-to-day things and praying that someday life will make sense again.

Halloween came, with swarms of costumed kids and their parents visiting the Store for Trick or Treat, cider and donuts on the porch. Lots of photos. Cute babies. Giggling children.

But, for us, grief had painted everything grey. The world remained out of synch.

By Thanksgiving week, I was glad to be occupied in receiving all sorts of Christmas merchandise, unpacking and displaying cards, toys and ornaments, while doing a steady business selling wine for turkey dinners and keeping plenty of baking supplies on hand.

In an effort to cheer myself, I ordered bouquets of fresh flowers, thinking we all might want a little reminder of what spring was like, once upon a time. By Thanksgiving Eve, I had sold all but two bouquets, and I congratulated myself that I had made a good call; my customers appreciated the idea of fresh flowers.

Just before closing, one of my regulars stopped in for a bottle of wine to bring to his mother's house the next day. He wanted a little help, so we picked out a nice Sauvignon Blanc and a Beaujolais Nouveau that had just come in.

As I started to ring up the charge, he grabbed the remaining two bouquets of flowers. "Can you wrap these up kind of nice for me? They're for someone very special." Well, of course. I selected some pretty tissues and ribbons, wrapped up the flowers and handed them to my handsome young customer.

"Oh, that looks great." He walked around the counter, placed the flowers in my arms and hugged me. "Happy Thanksgiving."

And, with a big smile and a wave, he was on his way into the early dark.

There are moments in one's life.

The winter lasts so long, it's so bleak. You think that maybe this time, the trees have completely forgotten how to bring forth leaves. There will never be another blossom.

You will never again give yourself up to laughter. The world will always be one or another shade of dreary.

But then, there it is. Completely unexpected. Unannounced. A kind gesture, a touch, a word. A miracle happens. A little light breaks through. Color is born anew.

It may be the smallest thing. But, it's enough.

Kyle and the Cat

It took a while to find someone to do the work of schlepping sodas and all sorts of grocery items from the basement storeroom to the selling floor. Also, taking care of the trash, the cardboard and other manual tasks around the store.

I don't remember exactly how I came to know Kyle. It was his sister, Jessie, at first, I think. A little older, a tiny little thing and a bundle of energy. She and Kyle kind of job shared for a little while until she got her driver's license and then she was on to bigger things. Kyle stayed though, longer than I ever expected him to.

A skinny, lanky young teen, into himself, pants practically falling off him. That was the style then; what were they thinking! When Kyle spoke, it was that slow, barely audible mumble that is characteristic of suburban boys trying to seem uninterested, bored but at the same time, kind of mad at the world. In the early part of his 'career' at the Store, I think he may have smiled a few times. Certainly not enough to make it a habit.

He always seemed to be in some kind of trouble that wasn't really his fault. I had a soft spot in my heart for him, and really believed that one of these days he was going to wake up and realize he had something to offer to the world, and to himself.

"Are you all done, Kyle?" Yeah. "Are you sure? Checked all the drinks. Coffees filled in. All the trash cans? Cardboard – including the basement. Sure?"

He thinks again, "Uhh. Yeah. Wait a minute. Oh. My bad. I'll be right back." He leaves - I don't know why, but I assume that my probing ignited some vague memory of a task undone. Or doors left unlocked. Who knows? Time passes. I genuinely have no idea where he went.

It's a quiet late summer afternoon - a weekday. The Post Office is closed for its mid-day siesta, so there aren't many customers around. I busy myself unpacking some of the candy boxes Kyle has brought up and left on the floor.

Suddenly, the front door flies open, and it's Kyle, animated beyond recognition. "Do you have any cat food? It's my cat! He ran away last night and he's out in the woods behind the Store! I gotta catch him."

He grabs a box of cat food from a lower shelf and books it out the back door, leaping over the deck railing, heading for the woods.

"Slow down! You're going to scare him off, Kyle!" I stand on the deck, hollering at the trees. No response. I wait. Nothing but crickets, and again I have no idea where he is. Luring the cat, I imagine. So I go back inside, to continue candy duty.

With Hershey Bars in hand, I look out the front window to see Kyle "carrying" an extremely agitated cat, which is hissing and howling to beat the band. Claws lashing out at whatever is in the way - in this case, Kyle's shirt, face and arms. This cat is not happy.

"You stupid, @#*^#*% cat!" A litany of expletives better left unprinted ensues. And, of course, the cat gets away, tearing down the porch and back to the safety of the woods.

Kyle drags himself in from the battle, covered with sweat, shredded shirt and bloodied arms. He is livid. But not beaten. "Do you have a box? I have to put him into something!"

How about taking your sweatshirt and wrapping him up in it so he can't do any further damage to you physically?

"Good idea."

He grabs his sweatshirt and hightails it out the back door again, flying over the deck railing. As he disappears into the trees once again, he yells over his shoulder, "Hey, Sherry! Can you call my Dad? Tell him I found the cat. Tell him to bring the car down so we can get him home!" He is on a mission.

Okay. I go back into the store and call the number for Kyle's house. His Dad answers, and I deliver the request.

An odd silence, then: "Our cat?" Yes, Kyle's out back trying to catch him. "Our cat?" Yes, that's right.

"Our cat is right here, sleeping on the floor." My turn for an awkward pause. Are you sure? Of course he's sure.

I go back out on the deck, staring at trees and I hear him out there - cursing the cat that has assaulted him and, at the same time, he is so determined to 'rescue'.

"Kyle?" I call out to the disembodied cursing voice.

"Kyle?" More cursing, more snapping of twigs.

"WHAT? Did you get my Dad?"

Uh, yes. "Kyle. That's not your cat."

"What?"

"That's not your cat, Kyle. Your cat is at home, asleep."

Silence.

"This isn't my cat?" Nope. "Are you sure?" Yep.

A bit later, he's standing in front of me, the fallen warrior. The cat won. They usually do. "That sure looked like my cat."

I gather sympathy. "I guess so. Maybe you should go home and clean up. Some ointment on those wounds, change your shirt? "

Ah. He means well.

The Rock Star

If they could see him now. The ROCK STAR.
World famous lead singer of one of the greatest
rock 'n roll bands in music history. Flamboyant,
effusive, a huge voice, that one of a kind mouth
that easily spreads into a one of a kind smile
covering most of his body.

This early Saturday morning, he's out for a run
wearing gym pants and a ratty grey sweatshirt.
Though the spectacular rings are still there. And,
there's that hair. And the sunglasses. Yep, even
without all the glamour and glitz, he can't be
mistaken for an ordinary citizen.

Today, though, he is doing an ordinary thing. He's
just a guy out for a run, stopping into my Store for
a cup of coffee and a muffin.

He's safe here – free from the craziness of stardom.
This is off the record. This is home. It's true that
here – usually – no one really bothers him. This
may be one of the biggest reasons he likes to live in
our little tucked away Victorian village. He's an
accepted part of the scenery.

Sure, people like to wave and give a 'howdy' to the Village Main Event. "Hey Steven! When's the next tour?" And, he does love to chat it up with the neighbors. It's also true that, wherever he is, it's impossible to ignore his presence.

His personality just fills the space. Even in a reflective mood, even in this rare nonverbal moment, his aura of Fourth of July sparklers is palpable.

He takes a huge bite of the muffin and makes all sorts of appreciative sounds, nodding enthusiastically. Blueberry. His favorite.

I ring up the sale, but of course he has no cash with him. Not a problem. Long ago, he set up his system with me. When he's got some money, he gives me a bunch that I keep in a plastic margarine cup in the safe under the counter. That way, he's covered for purchases when he's not carrying cash.

"Thanks, Steven. Have a good run. Say 'hi' to Theresa for me." And he's out the door, taking a left and walking down to the end of the porch, sipping his coffee as he meanders down our quiet, tree-lined street with all its lovely old homes.

I did say that 'usually' no one bothers him.

"Was that … HIM?" Jim bursts into the front door, fairly destroying the morning's peaceful tone. "Yes. You missed him again."

This guy has been trying to get face time with Steven for years. Once, he staged a sit-in on the front porch for hours, claiming he would not leave until he met Steven. I warned him that approach was probably not going to yield the desired result, that Steven was not 'regular' in that regard and could not be predicted. He wouldn't hear of it. He sat at the table on the porch until it was well after dark. I guess his wife was looking for him and someone came to take him home.

"DAMN! I can't BELIEVE it!" Jim stands in the middle of the Store as though he's just realized he threw away a winning lottery ticket. "What if I just run after him?" He says that, but he's glued to the floor just inside the front door. He wants – desperately – to meet him, but running madly down the street? Might just make a fool of himself. Not cool. And, one does not want to be uncool with an international ROCK STAR.

So, he stands there, frozen in the moment when he almost met his hero.

"I don't understand it, really," I tell him. "Most everyone in the neighborhood has met him –

either here, or at the movies, at the supermarket, or on the road when he's out for a walk, or at one of his kids' school things. It's too bad, really - you being such a big fan and all."

Jim hangs his head, as though acknowledging a personal failing. "I guess I'll just get my coffee. And the *Globe*." I detect a resigned sigh. He lingers a moment longer and then turns his back to me as he prepares his coffee.

His shoulders labored, hair slightly greyer, his mumble almost imperceptible. "I can't believe it." He stirs his coffee with the little stick, stops a moment (was that another sigh?), then stirs some more. Finally, he makes his way to the counter, gathering his dignity.

Pity overtakes me. I reach into the safe, take out the margarine cup and cradle it in my hand, reverently.

"Would you like to hold his private money stash for a minute?" He looks at me in disbelief. "No way!" "Yes, way." He gently fingers the yellow and blue plastic cup with 'Steven' written across it in magic marker.

A touch closer to his idol, he beams.

Elisha

I've told this story to very few people. And I understand that there are those reading who will find it....well, odd. I thought a lot before including this story, but it's an important part for me, so here goes.

Back in the early '80s, I heard about a man who was a renowned Trans-Medium, living in Western Massachusetts. Although, I didn't really know what a Trans-Medium was, I was no stranger to 'New Age' folks of all sorts - Psychics, Tarot Card readers, Mystics.

I was open to a new adventure, so I called and made an appointment. In a few weeks, on a very rainy day in early autumn, I traveled out to the woods west of Boston and found my way to the home of Mr. Elwood Babbitt, a very affable and unassuming gentleman, offering tea and welcome.

We sat in his living room, he in a deep upholstered chair and I on the sofa. "Here's what is going to happen" he began. "We'll sit here for a bit in the quiet, and then it will appear as though I've fallen asleep."

"Then, in due time, Dr. Fischer will come and talk with you. You may ask him anything you like, but he'll also have some things to tell you."

I had done a little research; I knew that Dr. Fischer had lived in England, in another time, and was one of the 'entities' that spoke through Mr. Babbitt. I couldn't imagine how he was going to manage making contact, but I was fascinated.

Just as he had described, in fairly short order he seemed to fall sound asleep, right there in his comfy chair. I waited patiently. Enough time passed that I began to wonder if anything was going to happen. Then, as surely as if the door had opened - which it had not – I felt someone come into the room. I couldn't see whoever it was, but I could most definitely feel the presence.

Within moments, Mr. Babbitt opened his eyes, looked at me and spoke. I realized that whoever was talking to me was absolutely NOT Elwood Babbitt, but rather was using Mr. Babbitt's physical body, perhaps like a really skilled ventriloquist!

He introduced himself, "My name is Dr. Fischer."

I'm not making this up, you know. I was stone sober, and do not use drugs. This really happened.

Now you see why I don't tell many people?

For the next hour or so, Dr. Fischer told me things about the world, history, life on other planets (oh yes) and, as Mr. Babbitt had explained, he told me about myself.

I had lived many lives, and one in particular, in Victorian times, was to become quite relevant to me in this lifetime.

There was so much information, I was glad that Mr. Babbitt had insisted I tape the experience. When I got back home, I transcribed the tape, then packed everything in a box and went on with my life.

Like I said, I told very few people about my experience. Unless one has gone through this kind of thing, it's pretty hard to imagine, much less believe.

Years went by and, though the experience itself made a real impression on me, the specifics of the session became a distant, vague memory.

One Sunday afternoon, a few years into our new life as General Store owners, I was cleaning out my attic at home and came across the box with the audiotape and transcriptions from my session with

Mr. Babbitt/Dr. Fischer. Literally, a voice from the past. I was curious and started to read.

About half way through, I came to the part where he had told me about past lives and that one of them was to 'become relevant to me in this lifetime.'

"In Victorian times, you were a merchant and your name was Elisha. Besides being a successful business man, you were active in your community, which was very important to you."

I stopped cold.
My house. My store.
Elisha's house! Elisha's store!

Is it even possible that, in a past life, *he* had been *me?*

Who knows?

Kind of rolls around in the mind, though.

Doesn't it?

Christmas

Every year, I so looked forward to Christmas. As if it wasn't enough that I had my beautiful Victorian across the street to decorate – I had the store and, in many ways, I enjoyed that even more. After all, it's where I LIVED now. And, this was where all my friends came to see me. By comparison, the house was lonely.

Bringing Christmas spirit to the Store was easy and gratifying. Garland was draped all around the inside and outside, on the railings and columns, as well as across the top of the porch. Little white lights everywhere. Wreaths on every door and a live tree on the porch.

The whole building glowed like a hearth in the middle of the village.

Stocking up for the holiday was like a great big shopping excursion. It was important to me that we sold all the old-fashioned Christmas candies, cookies and eggnog. For a few years, we took orders for pies. I'd bake them at home, box them up and bring them across the street for customers to pick up. Can't remember when I had so much fun.

I grew up in New England in the '50s and, like so many of us in the 'Boomer' generation, had warm memories of Christmas past, in what seemed like a simpler time. I remembered the little log cabins with Balsam incense in the chimneys that my grandmother had on her mantle. Balsam sachet pillows. Caroler candles.

I wanted all of those things on my shelves.

We sold nostalgic Christmas CDs with Bing Crosby and Gene Autry, Ribbon Candy and hand knitted mittens. We had stuffed bears with Santa hats and metal fire engines. Stocking stuffers like Jax and jump ropes.

I found interesting contemporary gifts too; a big favorite was the collection of Willow Tree Angels, those oddly beautiful faceless figures whose body language conveyed so much meaning. Boy, we sold a lot of those.

One year, I made custom hand painted ornaments and custom retro candy gift boxes. My imagination ran wild! Did I mention I had a lot of fun?

This was the time of year – between Thanksgiving and Christmas – when a lot of distant family members returned to the neighborhood. So, there were many faces we didn't recognize coming in the door. They may have been unfamiliar to us, but the Store was very familiar to them.

It was wonderful hearing stories about growing up down the street, and coming to the Store every day after school. "The candy was right there – in the same corner." There was a lot of talk about sitting on the stone wall across the street. That was where a lot of the kids used to hang out. On the wall.

Entire families came in to see what we'd done with the place and always, always were so happy to find that the Store was still there.

One rather cold, blustery Sunday afternoon just before Christmas, a man I had never seen before walked into the store to get a cup of coffee. He was feeling kind of low because he was headed to the Mall to shop for gifts. He hated the Mall. He hated shopping. So, we got to talking about his 'list' and we got to poking around the store and finding some things that just might make a great present for this niece or that brother.

Before we knew it, we were done! Gifts for everyone. He sat down at the table in the front of the store and had another cup of coffee while I wrapped every one of those gifts, loaded them into shopping bags and then sent him on his way.

He was SO happy! One of my best days, ever.

I thoroughly enjoyed helping people choose gifts, particularly when the kids came in to find a treasure for mom or dad. Truth be told, I stayed open on Christmas Eve as long as possible, because I just had such a great sense of satisfaction when a frazzled customer came in at the last minute and needed something for someone. I felt like Santa Claus.

To make it perfect, if we were under a lucky star, there would be snow. Not like the mean blizzards of mid winter, no. I'm talking about the gentle, exhilarating first snows that dress up all the leftover dead leaves, that glisten in the street lights, that make the earth seem like a peaceful and intimate place to be.

Sometimes, it was pure magic.

The

"Rest of the Story"

Lest you get the idea that I wore rose colored glasses for all those years at the Store, let me tell you there were times when I seriously wanted to leave on the next plane.

It never occurred to me that running such a small business would be so much work. So much mind numbing, back breaking, nerve-racking WORK. Customers saw the fun part – being behind the counter, chatting it up with friends, wrapping a gift. Oh sure.

What they didn't see were the hours in front of my computer in my office – paying bills, doing QuickBooks reports (well, after it took me forever to learn QuickBooks!), finding vendors, placing orders, dealing with the Lottery, etc.

Of course, running any business has its challenges. And, having the best little store in the best little neighborhood was no exception.

Take the weather. We're in New England, so the concept of seasons is not new. We know what it is to deal with weather extremes. But, owning the Store gave new meaning to "SNOW? AGAIN?" and "WILL THIS HEAT WAVE NEVER END?"

I remember one winter when it seemed to snow – a lot – every single day. We were lucky enough to have Ken, a great and devoted plow guy, who I could hear plowing our parking lot long before anyone else was up. But, when the snow keeps on coming, you just run out of places to put it! There were days when the drifts piled up on the front porch so deep, we couldn't open the front door. What fun!

So, you think: Summer. That would sure be nice. However, if it's close to 100 degrees and you know there's a delivery of frozen food coming – 'sometime' today – you will spend the day watching for that truck. When it arrives and those big boxes are unloaded onto the hot pavement, you are hustling your buns to get everything into the basement and into the freezers.

Heaven forbid freezers should break down - which they did - and boxes of muffin dough, ice cream and other goodies would need to be thrown out. Oh, that happened with coolers too. Milk. Cream. Yogurt. Out.

Okay. So, those are admittedly extreme situations. What about the more ordinary, daily things? Remember that old time popcorn machine that I ordered around 3:00 AM one night before we opened? Wonderful! So cute! Smelled great! Everyone loved having fresh popcorn.

Well. Ever try to clean one of those babies? All that oil on the plastic windows? Yes, yes, they sell product for that. Hmmm. At one point, I tried an electronic steamer. Hmmm. Really makes you appreciate microwave.

Those fabulous Bongi Turkey Pies that everyone loved? Guess what? Bongi's is several miles away, down in Duxbury and they do not deliver. So, every week, I'm driving to Bongi's and loading up boxes of frozen pies into my station wagon. Heavy. Good thing I was young then!

Most vendors do deliver. Hopefully. But, what happens when key vendors decide your store just isn't big enough to be bothered with? Who's going to bring you Twinkies? And chips? And bread? Answer: go get it yourself! BJ's Wholesale Club became a second home.

Admittedly, some of our challenges were self-inflicted. All right, a lot of them. Like – expansion!

Not far into the ownership of the Store, we decided we just didn't have enough room. We needed groceries. We needed beer and wine. We needed more ice cream. We needed an addition. Research into what we had for lot lines revealed that we could add three feet along the north side of the building, a small room fitting into an existing corner and a back deck. Not much. But, more space is more space. And, in retail, space is everything.

The construction of all that was such a project, I think I blocked it from memory. My husband was in charge of this undertaking, so I was able to suspend consciousness until it was completed and I then found myself stocking the wall of groceries and lining up the lovely bottles of wine.

I loved our wine room – and our customers loved being able to buy their dinner wine right down the street, rather than driving a few miles to the nearest big store. Sadly, there were no year-round licenses available at the time, and we were able to obtain only a *seasonal* beer and wine license. This meant we had to stop selling mid January and begin again April 1. No one liked this arrangement. But, there it was. For a few months each winter, our wine room was empty and our coffers depleted.

Then there are the things we tried that didn't work at all! Bob talked me into the concept of hand scooped ice cream cones. So, we created a space for the ice cream freezer – the kind you place big tubs of ice cream in, and then use a scooper to make a lovely ice cream cone. Terrific idea! Except (why is there so often an 'except'?) what happens when there's only one person at the register – which is ALWAYS – and someone wants an ice cream cone? The law of physics claims that a person cannot be in more than one place at one time, and I am here to tell you, that's a fact.

Then there was that one tiny detail involving running out of a flavor and needing to go outside, around to the basement, into the BIG freezer, heft a big tub of ice cream and bring it back upstairs. Remember: there's ONE person minding the store! People are waiting up there. Waiting. Patiently.

Did that last a year? I don't think so. The ice cream freezer was removed, leaving a big rust mark on the hardwood floor that is there to this day. We covered it with a nice braided rug.

Cardboard? We couldn't bring ourselves to put all those tons of cardboard (I never saw so much cardboard in my life!) in the trash. That would be an eco disaster.

So, every week, we broke it down and brought it to the dump to recycle. Until we finally got smart and got a recycle bin to sit so nicely right next to the trash bin and let Waste Management take care of it.

Like I said, a lot of our challenges were our own doing. Our hearts were in the right place, but we were so naïve, in many ways!

It's funny. These memories didn't come rushing to the fore when I started writing down my Store stories. I suspect it's something like childbirth, that your mind, in self-preservation, protects you from the memory of pain. Now that I've primed the pump, there's a kind of slideshow going on in my head – vivid images of things that just did not work or went horribly wrong.

Now, where did I put those rose colored glasses?

Star of the Day

Years from now, the little General Store in the center of our village will still be there. Some well - intended soul will be stocking the candy corner and making recommendations on what wine to buy. Every morning, a Charlie will arrive early and buy a lottery ticket, a cup of coffee and maybe a muffin. Preoccupied young men will leave their cars running while they dash in and pay for a newspaper. Kids will get off the school bus and pile into the store with way too much energy. Lively white haired widows will look for greeting cards. Young moms will bring in their toddlers to buy a pop.

Occasionally, maybe on a holiday weekend, folks will stop in and the owner won't recognize them. They don't live in the neighborhood, but they 'used to'. They will walk around, smile and say, "Wow, I haven't been here since I was a kid. I used to buy candy here – right in this corner, just like this."

They'll ask the owner how long he or she has owned the store, and then they'll talk about the way it was – years ago.

"There was this woman who used to own the store. Her name was Sherry. She was nice, and she didn't seem to mind all us kids. I remember she made me 'do the math' whenever I bought something. She would say, "If you can't add it up, you can't buy it." I guess it really bugged her that kids in those days couldn't add in their heads! And, if you took out money from your pocket – or your shoe – and it was all crumpled up, she'd hand it back to you and make you flatten it out, nice and smooth, and hand it back to her. She was funny that way. But, you know, the thing I remember most about her was her dog…"

Her dog. That lovely pale Golden Retriever, perfectly named Star. She was there when Sherry was there. If you saw Star lying on the front porch or across the front door (so everyone coming in had to step over her), you knew Sherry was behind the counter. They were a team.

Star's job was to be wonderful, the object of love and adoration.

She was there for every toddler who wanted to bury his face in her abundant fur. She was there to offer solace to every tired guy at the end of a long day at work. She was there to remind everyone who was drawn into her sphere of influence that unconditional love isn't just a phrase and that oh, well, I guess life can't be all that bad.

There truly was something special about this dog.

Before becoming a permanent fixture at the Store, Star was a visiting dog at a local nursing home. Weaving her magic web, she cast a spell of comfort and warmth among the lonely residents, occasionally performing a tiny miracle like inspiring a mute stroke victim to speak his first words in months. *"What a beautiful dog!" he said, stroking her silky ears.*

"Star of the Day, who will it be?" Ray Amorosi sang to her whenever he walked through the door to find her holding court. She was always the Star of the Day.

It was late fall in 2008, just before Sherry sold the Store. Star was diagnosed with brain tumors and began to fail. Less than a year, the vet said. Unsteady and sometimes more than a little wobbly, Star came to the Store every day. She would hear the keys as Sherry picked them up from the kitchen counter, and she'd wake up from her nap, slowly getting to her feet, going to the door prepared to walk across the street – like every other day.

Once at the Store, she assumed her place – blocking traffic – and went back to sleep, stirring only for a familiar touch.

When, on one November afternoon, there was a
sign on the front door of the Store "closed
temporarily" there were some who intuitively knew
what had happened. Beloved Star had died. At
home, lying in the sun, with Sherry holding her
and stroking her face.

It's probably best that, a very short time after,
Sherry turned over the Store to new owners. Being
there without Star was just too painful. Though,
she was not the only one who was heartbroken –
even grown men broke down in tears when they
came in expecting to see the ever present Star. It
would never be the same without her. It was the
end of an era.

*"I guess everyone thinks that their childhood was special and
that nothing could ever be like that again. But, you know, I
think that being a kid here, at that time, coming to the store
every day... Sherry scolding me for not knowing how to add
up my money – because she really cared – that was pretty
great. And that dog. Everyone loved her dog. And everyone
loved her loving her dog."*

"Star" by Wiesy MacMillan

Hollywood Ending

On Tuesday morning, December 7, 2008, I was startled awake by the phone at 6:00 o'clock. It was a reporter from *The Patriot Ledger* asking me to verify a news piece that appeared in that morning's edition of *The Boston Globe*. "Is it true that you have sold the Marshfield Hills General Store to Steve Carell, the actor?" Yes. It's true. Amazingly. Oddly. Mysteriously. True.

By mid morning, Channel 7 News was set up at the Store: lights, camera, action. Later in the day, Fox News showed up. The phone rang constantly – every radio station, wanting details. "Is he going to work behind the counter?" *Of course.*

The sale of a mid-1800's building, off the beaten path on the South Shore of Boston ordinarily would not be newsworthy. But, a movie star buying a little antique building with a post office and country store, now that's a story!

It happened so fast. We all had made the decision to sell the building and had listed it with Janet Koelsch, our Realtor. Things had changed, lives were taking different paths. It was time.

Letting go of the Store, on the other hand, oh....I just wasn't ready for that. There had been suitors and I had felt tempted, but I just couldn't imagine myself without the comfort of my little center of the world, my place in the neighborhood. I was prepared to stay on and continue paying rent to the new owners, whoever they would be, and run my Store for who knows how long.

Then, on a Sunday afternoon in mid-October, I walked in the Store's front door to prepare for the day's closing and found my friend and neighbor Tish Vivado waiting for me. She had a question. "Is it true the building is for sale?" Why, yes it is, actually. "And the Store?" No, it's not.

She continued. "My brother-in-law wants to make an investment and he loves this building. He may be interested." Okay. Well, that's great. "You know who my brother-in-law is, right?" No, can't say as I do. "He's Steve Carrell, the actor."

Wow. Steve Carell? "Dan in Real Life"? "The Office"? Wow. This is very interesting. I gave her Janet's number and said, "Give her a call and we'll see what happens."

Tuesday night, Janet called. "Expect an offer tomorrow morning." Wow again. That was fast!

"But, here's the other shoe: they won't buy the building unless you also sell your business. The plan is for Tish to manage the Store for him."

I didn't want to let go. But, Fate was whistling at me again. He loves the neighborhood; he's from the area. He has respect for history. He cares about the Store. He will take it beyond where I ever would be able to. It's a great opportunity – good for the business, good for the neighborhood. It's the right thing to do. Take a breath. Okay.

Within two weeks, we were signing the deal and in almost no time, Bob and I were standing in the basement with the building inspector and Steve Carell. He is so real, so kind, so sincere - I trust him. And, Tish is so full of energy and ideas. I trust them to take care of my 'baby'.

So, now we're a national news item! Everybody is all excited. Marshfield Hills is on the map. Google is filled with links to Steve Carell and The Marshfield Hills General Store! He talks about it on the Red Carpet at the Golden Globe Awards, for heaven's sake! Didn't see this one coming.

My little store. My little world. Not mine anymore.

Marshfield Hills GENERAL STORE

New Years Eve

We had a lovely snow yesterday. No wind. Not too cold. Just a couple of inches, leaving behind coated branches and, as dark approached, the lingering echoes of children sledding down our small hills.

A few of us from the neighborhood decided to gather at Sands End, a local beach bistro, open for dinner this one night during its winter respite. Weighted with the changes of this past year, we were subdued and reflective.

Noisemakers lay dormant on the tables. Music, low and nostalgic.

After dinner, our little group left early. There were light parting kisses and murmured well wishes, as we went our separate ways.

Another dusting of snow had fallen. *Snow on snow.*

A rare Blue Moon shone incandescent and the landscape glowed.

I say a prayer of gratitude for the year that delivered us here, to this blessed silence. With equanimity, we gently brush off the residue of spent hours. Missions accomplished.

Disappointments swallowed. Broken hearts.

Miracles.

And, in this silence - in this quiet hour - we wait.

In this quiet hour, we wait

To breathe the cold, fresh air

Of new beginnings,

Fragrant with possibility.

~ Since

Dear Reader,

Within a year after relinquishing ownership of the Store, we sold our beautiful Victorian house across the street, as well. We decided it was time for a different lifestyle and warmer climates, so we moved our main residence to Punta Gorda, Florida; we still maintain a summer home in Scituate.

Leaving the Hills involved a lot of tears, and it took some time to find new direction and new inspiration. With our little dog Boo, we have traveled throughout the Western U.S., the Bahamas and Mexico and are planning more travel in the near future now that grandchildren are scattered everywhere!

I have become a Certified Yoga Teacher and freelance writer. Bob has achieved his Captain's license and become a Master Gardener in Florida.

So, the lesson is well learned – life continues to unfold its mysteries and surprises. We only need to be open to receive and something wonderful will happen!

With much love,

Sherry

A note of thanks to ~

Molly, Patty, Wiesy, Norton, Jessie, Kyle,
Brooks and Hank for being more than employees –
we were family!

My husband, Bob, for his partnership in the Store.
Without him, it would not have been possible.

Dave Will for his lovely Cover Photo and several
candid photographs within the book

David Brega for helping to make the book beautiful

Sally Dean for her charming Candy Corner artwork

Wiesy MacMillan for her portraits of Brooks & Star

Viola Khumen for the Back Cover Photo

Cynthia Krusell, Historical Research Associates for
the vintage photographs of Marshfield Hills

Ray Amorosi for his steady friendship & vision

Colleen Clopton for her editorial support

Richard Wainwright for sharing his wisdom

Sharon Whitehill and the Friday morning writers'
group in Punta Gorda for encouraging me to write!

David Cohen of Smith Print for his skill, sensitivity
and compassion

Steve Carell and Tish Vivado for their tender,
loving care of the Store and carrying it forward into
the next generation.

Village Images ~

Village Images ~

First page, left to right:

Marci Littlefield, Claire Robinson, Linda Sordillo, Sherry Bechtold
North Community Church
Old Goat Lapel Pin
Rick Larson with Tai
Patty Mulkearn
Hannah Larson with Arrow
Dave Will
Viola Khumen
Old Bell at Church Cemetery
Brad White
Clift Rogers Library
Wiesy MacMillan
J Michael Sullivan
Exhibition at The Arts Festival

Second page, left to right:

The Pink Victorian and Star
Steven Tyler and David Brega
Amber Gross, Mal Noonan, Janet Kastrud, Marie Kermin,
        Suzie O'Gara, Susan Robinson, Meghan Peck
Taylor Singer and Champ
Ray Amorosi
Doug Aaberg
Bob Norton
Molly Singer (Putnam)
Bob Bechtold

Third and Fourth pages: Neighborhood kids at the Store - Halloween

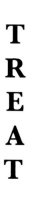

T R I C K   O R   T R E A T

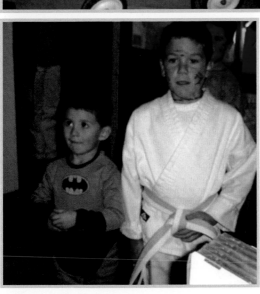

2
0
0
3